I0147314

James Spencer Northcote, Charles Meynell

The 'Colenso' controversy considered from the Catholic standpoint

Being five letters about Dr. Colenso's work upon the Pentateuch

James Spencer Northcote, Charles Meynell

The 'Colenso' controversy considered from the Catholic standpoint
Being five letters about Dr. Colenso's work upon the Pentateuch

ISBN/EAN: 9783337268411

Printed in Europe, USA, Canada, Australia, Japan

Cover: Foto ©Lupo / pixelio.de

More available books at **www.hansebooks.com**

THE 'COLENSO' CONTROVERSY

CONSIDERED FROM THE

CATHOLIC STANDPOINT;

BEING

FIVE LETTERS

ABOUT

DR. COLENSO'S WORK UPON THE PENTATEUCH,

AND THE CRITICISMS WHICH IT HAS CALLED
FORTH ON EITHER SIDE.

BY

THE VERY REV. CANON NORTHCOTE, D.D.,

PRESIDENT OF ST. MARY'S COLLEGE, OSCOTT;

AND

THE REV. C. MEYNELL, D.D.,

PROFESSOR OF MENTAL PHILOSOPHY IN THE SAME COLLEGE.

LONDON:
THOMAS RICHARDSON AND SON,
26, PATERNOSTER ROW; 9, CAPEL STREET, DUBLIN; AND DERBY.
MDCCCLXIII.

PREFACE.

A few words of explanation are necessary as to the shape in which the materials of this little publication have been cast by its authors. The first letter was written *bonâ fide* and without any view to publication : but the epistolary form in the others was chosen, *as a convenient fiction*, by means of which the writers were enabled to address two very different classes of persons who were likely to be affected by Dr. Colenso's mischievous publication. The letters themselves bear witness that there never was any real disagreement between their respective writers, as to the management of the controversy : but since each of them had taken a different view of it, and adopted a distinct line of argument, they gladly seized upon what seemed the only method of working together, as they hope, for the general good. The facility, also, of the epistolary style was a great advantage to persons writing as they have written under the pressing burden of various other duties.

Feb. 7, 1863.
St. Mary's College, Oscott.

THE 'COLENSO' CONTROVERSY

CONSIDERED FROM THE

CATHOLIC STANDPOINT.

LETTER I.

Dear Doctor,

I wish to have your opinion about a matter which has always been interesting to me, and which certain recent publications have made a subject of importance—the attitude I mean of the *faithful* mind towards difficulties and objections which may be urged against the truths of religion.

Some persons seem to think that it is in the power of the Catholic apologist to give a direct and satisfactory answer to every possible objection which may be started against the Christian religion, lest error seem to triumph. But (if you will agree with me) I am persuaded that this statement of the case is absolutely inadmissible. Very many objections, it is true, demand and admit of such a reply; but others (and on the whole, I should say the far greater number) are *directly* unanswerable; though in every case (I ought to add) these admit of course, a sufficient *indirect* answer. Now it is a point of wisdom that the controversialist should be practically conscious of this truth, which, when clearly laid before him, I think he will hardly venture to deny. Where the question is, mainly, one of fact, truth is always successful against falsehood, learning against ignorance, and profoundness against shallow brilliancy. The "End of Controversy," and the "Lectures on the Holy Eucharist," have for this reason proved superior to attack; because, in those days, the question was not so much a matter of *reason* as a matter of *fact*. It was asked, whether this or that doctrine were really contained, or implied in that Divine page which both parties equally reverenced as inspired? such as—"Whether or not the Scriptures declare themselves to be a sufficient Rule of Faith? Whether or not such doctrines as the

Supremacy of St. Peter, the Infallibility of the Church, the Real Presence, Auricular Confession, were countenanced or condemned in Holy Writ? and so forth. I do not mean to say that questions of reason were never brought into the controversy: for they were brought in. But I speak of the general tenour of the discussion. It was about matters of fact; and the task of the controversialist, however laborious, was not perplexed as it now is, when the question has become one of the reason. There was always to be found somewhere or other a direct solution of the difficulty—a straight-forward answer to a straight-forward question. But it has become far otherwise now that the difficulties are of the reason.

I should beware of meeting directly such questions as " How can God be at once Three Persons and yet one God? How could God the Son—*the same Person*—at once know and not know the Day of Judgment?—How can the same body, as in the Holy Eucharist, be in many places at once?—If any man really knows *how* these things can be so, he is wiser than I. I am aware that direct answers to such questions are furnished by the schoolmen, for the purpose of making the matter as intelligible as it can be made. I own that such answers have their use in this respect. But do they fully satisfy the objection? This I cannot admit. For the Holy Trinity is a *mystery*, which it would not be if I knew *how* God is one God, and yet Three Persons : the Incarnation of God the Son is a mystery, which it would not be if I could render it fully intelligible how the same Person could, in this case, know and not know the same thing. I was always better pleased with the indirect answers, less ambitious but more really effective—such as the analogy of the Holy Trinity and the Human Soul; that of the union of the Divine and Human Natures in Christ, and the union of a soul and body in man ; the presence of the Body of Christ in the Holy Eucharist, and that of the soul in the body—wholly in the whole and again wholly in each part, as St. Thomas teaches from Aristotle.

But, perhaps, a more effective method than all, in dealing with an unbeliever who finds the Christian Doctrines contradictory is this :—" Better come to another matter," I would say; " Would you, or would you not accept these doctrines, if (believing there is a God of truth) you knew that He asked you and commanded you to accept them? Would you dare thus answer *Him*, that they were contradictions and that you could not accept them? Is it likely, on the other hand, that God has left men to go their own ways? Has He not Himself spoken to man about what he is to believe, and how he is to worship?" —Thus bring the unbeliever to admit the necessity of some Divine Authority, such as the Catholic Church, and his difficulties will not vanish (of course they will not) but they will appear to him in a new light; and if he obtain the gift of faith, instead of being a subject of pain and disquiet, they will become incentives to humility and adoration. But if this be the case, is there not some waste of labour over difficulties which must still remain after the objector is converted? And would not much of this labour be better spent in sounding the inquirer's state of mind, and reading his own heart to him? For I am persuaded that the minds of many of these " *earnest Truth-seekers*" (as they style themselves) are in an attitude of unconscious rebellion against God.—" I am as free in my way as He is in His. I have a right to know good reasons—reasons which I think satisfactory for what He bids me believe ; and if He condemns me on this head, let Him look to it." These are dreadful words, but they are, I firmly believe, the language of the heart of many such persons, who have some good left in them, and to whom it would do good to read, as I said, their own hearts to them, and to threaten them with the wrath which their *devilish* pride (I can find no better term) so richly deserves. —" I did not argue with him, *but I think I frightened him,*" said a friend of mine about an unbeliever with whom he had some words. Alas! how many well-meaning persons rush into disputes about matters to which they are unequal, and not only do not frighten, but get the worst of the argument into the bargain. Those who read " the papers" at this time, may witness some painful instances. It may well be asked whether Bishop Colenso's objections or the answers which they have called forth will do more harm.

But are the preceding remarks, then, applicable to the recent publication against the veracity of the Pentateuch? I think so. There is indeed a vast difference between Mysteries of Faith and those seeming inconsistencies which Dr. Colenso has pointed out in the Scripture narrative. The difficulty which the former present to the human reason is owing to the natural limitation of our thinking faculties ; while the latter, as matters invested with a merely accidental obscurity arising from deficient experience, are difficulties of a lower order altogether. And yet, however unlike in its nature and origin, a similar phenomenon manifests itself in both cases ; that is to say, in both cases it is a question of reconciling one portion of the Divine Message with another where we have not (clearly) the whole statement of the case laid before us. And the similarity of the phenomenon suggests a similarity of treatment. So here again I leave it to those who are wiser than I, to furnish direct answers to such questions as these—How can the Mosaic Record be reconciled with Sir Charles Lyell's principles of geology? How could Noe feed all the creatures in the Ark, such as beasts and birds which prey upon each other—swallows, bats, reptiles, insects, &c.? Or, How could the children of Phares (Hesron and Hamul) be born in Egypt, since they are numbered (Gen. xlvi.) amongst those who *went down* into Egypt? Or how could they have been born in the land of Canaan consistently with the facts recorded Gen. xxxviii.? How could a population of 2,000,000 have made the marches recorded in the time recorded? How could they have got food, where no miraculous agency is recorded; and when such miraculous agency is recorded, did the flocks and herds eat quails and manna too? Where did the Israelites get their arms from, with which they fought the Amalekites? How is it that at a census recorded Exod. xxx., the number of adult males should exactly tally with the number at a census taken six months later—Num. 1. whereas the ratio of increase ought to have been 215 (?) *per diem*? How get the number of fighting men 603,000, at the time of the Exodus, with a proportionate number of aged, females, and children amounting altogether to a population of 2,000,000, out of the twelve sons of Jacob and their wives, allowing the very highest probable ratio of increase? How can the conquests of the Israelites (considering the difficulties as to time and numbers) be made probable? How can the numerous and intricate duties of the priests have been punctually and faithfully discharged, according to the law? etc., etc.

Now, what I think specially noticeable in this sort of controversy is this; that whereas the difficulty is clear, patent, palpable, yet the answer is (and in most cases cannot be otherwise than) a mere supposition. And I do not say this, mind, out of any contempt for the answers, when they are sensible ones : yet such is the fact ; and we ought to be aware of it, and not to insist upon such direct answers (if we attempt them at all) as if they were really our strong point ; which they are not, and cannot be. For I do not *know* (no man surely does) how the Mosaic Record of Creation is reconcileable with certain geological facts : but I have a view upon the matter;—I hold some theory which is more or less consistent and probable. Thus, I hold the Augustinian theory of the days as *indefinite periods;* I like Buckland's theory; I stand by Cardinal Wiseman, or I side with Hengstenberg: and so forth. I do not *know* how Noe fed the beasts, fowls, and creeping things. But I *suppose* supernatural agency of one sort or another. God fed them—sustained them without food—taught Noe some (unknown) natural means of providing for their wants. I *suppose,* again, that the names of Hesron and Hamul were a gloss (to make up the number) which has crept into the text; or, that the writer inserted them in this case as "guided by genealogical, rather than historical considerations," or that some number in the original date of calculation has got altered. I *suppose* supernatural agency to meet various difficulties of the Exodus; that God strengthened the people to perform their various journies; supplied their wants oftentimes, and those of their flocks and herds by unrecorded miracles : or, I think that there is no *dignus vindice nodus* for supernatural agency save when recorded; and, then, must suppose facts and circumstances in the back ground, as to their journies, method of living, means of subsistence, acquisition of arms, and discipline on the march, which have not come down to us. I *suppose* that the census mentioned in *Exodus* and that in *Numbers* may possibly be the same census; and that the numbers were really taken when the tribute was paid, but not given in till six months afterwards; or that some unrecorded fact in the back ground would set all right. I *suppose* that inter-mar-riages with Egyptians (or others) and an offspring in special cases vastly over the European average (such as we read of in the East and in Southern Europe and America) would make void the calculations as to the ratio of increase of the Israelites ; and that circumstances unrecorded would similarly affect other estimates and calculations.

But enough ; I do not wish to answer Colenso in this manner ; so it is needless to pursue further this portion of my subject. Let us own it; these are not really *answers* to the objections, but mere inventions of the imagination, which seeks to render intelligible that which is (to our minds) unin-telligible. They are conjectures which may some of them be true perhaps, or partially true ; but of this we know nothing. Others, which seem plausible enough, may be (if we only knew the whole state of the case) very wide of the mark. When we add to this that objections of this kind may be mul-tiplied *ad infinitum;* that it is proverbially easier to ask ques-tions than to answer them ; that, oftentimes, the various answers cancel one another; and that sometimes they only lay one difficulty to start twenty others—I think the controversialist will pause ere he venture to take his stand on so unsubstantial a basis. Rather as before I would bring the matter to this decisive issue : " How if God commanded you to believe—say the history of the Exodus as narrated by Moses (or whomsoever you suppose was the author) in the Bible. Are you *so certain* that there is no error, nor misapprehension about the data on which these supposed inconsistencies are founded, that you would dare tell Him that you would not, could not believe ?" For once get the objector to admit that God has spoken to man ; that the Bible is the Word of God (which however cannot be proved from the Bible itself) and he must see these difficulties in a new light, though difficulties there will ever be. If he be not full of conceit, if he wishes to believe ; then, he may be assisted by indirect arguments. He should be reminded that these calculations (though they look so imposing) are in themselves of small moment, and the *data* on which they are founded is everything; that he is supposing himself, or his authority a competent judge of these *data, and that* in such matters as the creation of this world, the deluge, and a migration of people which claims to have been conducted by the special agency of God Himself thousands of years ago ; that it is but natural that the history of such events should exhibit apparent inconsistencies and contradictions, when facts that have happened in our own days, such as the *life of Napoleon III., the American War, the exploits of Garibaldi read impossible and absurd when summarily narrated ;* while the duties of the Roman Pontiff might appear equally impossible *on paper,* as those of the Jewish High Priest ; that even the direct answers to objections, imperfect as they are, yet since they show that men in our circumstances can conceive a way by which the difficulties may be toned down and the facts related brought within the range of possibility, have their use, and are an argument that what is possible in conception may be considered possible in itself. He should be reminded also how little are these objections against the veracity of the Pentateuch, compared with the overwhelming mass of evidence in its favour : and instead of being allowed to attack, he should be himself put upon the defensive. Let this suffice however. I do not wish really to answer Colenso, but rather to submit to you the method by which I think this sort of unbelievers should be met. I would willingly hear what you have to say upon the matter. Of one thing I am

fully persuaded, viz., that if my method of answering do no
good, at any rate it can do no harm; whereas I fear the majority of answers which are published, and no doubt a proportionate number of unpublished ones will do much harm.
1st. Because the writers *do not own the difficulties*, and thus
seem to be arguing *in bad faith*. 2nd. Because, by trying to
answer questions which are unanswerable, they suffer an ig-
nominious defeat; and thus lead the objector to believe that
he has the better cause. 3rdly. Because they lose their tem-
pers and use unpleasant and vituperative language—showing
plainly which side, at any rate, has the best of the argument.
4thly. Because they write with a certain conceit and *bump-
tiousness* (if I may use a slang term) which is unworthy of
Christians—though, here, however they are fairly matched on
the other side. Now if my answer is a poor one, at any rate
it does not pretend to be better than it is. If there are difficulties in the Scripture which we cannot quite explain away,
let us acknowledge them. We have abundance of reason for
believing notwithstanding.

Yours, Dear Doctor,
Very affectionately,
C. M.

LETTER II.

My dear Friend,

I have allowed your letter to remain too long unanswered.
The delay has been unintentional and unavoidable; but it
has brought with it this advantage, that I have had the
opportunity of seeing some of the answers which Colenso's
book has elicited, so that I can now fully appreciate your
fears lest these should do more harm than the publication
they are intended to refute. I feel certain that many
of them cannot fail to have this effect; in particular, those
which pretend to laugh at Colenso's difficulties, on the one
hand, and, on the other, those which go a long way in con-
ceding all that he contends for in his premises, and yet think
that they can deny his conclusion.

No doubt, Colenso's publication and its history present a
very tempting subject for ridicule to those who do not feel

keenly about the spiritual interests that may be endangered by it. It is very easy and very tempting to make a joke about "Colenso's Arithmetic applied to the Pentateuch," about a Protestant Bishop setting out with his Bible to convert the savages, "catching a Tartar," and being himself converted by these same savages so as to discard the Bible, or at least very considerably to lower its estimate in his own mind and in the minds of others. But when a writer goes beyond this, and says that the difficulties he has stated are childish and absurd, and "such as a Sunday-school girl might answer," he only betrays his own ignorance or insincerity. On the other hand, there have been writers who are not afraid to acknowledge that "Colenso has demonstrated a consistency in error pervading every part of the Exodus narrative, which absolutely forbids our accepting its Arithmetic in the form in which it is now presented to us," and yet seek to escape from his conclusion that the Book, so full of errors, is not to be trusted as a true narrative of historical facts. If in the former class of writers we desiderated more sincerity, in these we certainly want more logic; and both of one and the other we must needs confess—

Non tali auxilio, non defensoribus istis
Tempus eget.

Everyone must feel, that answers of this kind inflict a real injury upon the cause they are intended to serve; and if these are the only direct answers that can be given, better far to abstain from answering at all, or to give only that indirect form of answer which you recommend. Indeed there can be no doubt that the indirect answer is always safer, and often stronger, than any direct answer which it is possible to give. Nevertheless I do not think that in the present moment it would be quite sufficient. The indirect answer seems to me more effective as a preventive and precautionary measure than as a remedy ; more useful for the masses than for individuals. Let me explain what I mean. You know that not long since I had the charge of a large and intelligent, but on the whole an uneducated, congregation ; there was a fair sprinkling amongst them of young men, very fond of reading or "hearing some new thing." Had I continued to be their pastor during the last few months, I might very probably have considered it my duty to give them some few lectures on the general idea of a Divine Revelation ; on the Authority of the Church, on the Inspiration and Interpretation of Scripture, and in particular, on the credibility of the Old Testament.

In this course of Lectures, it would only have been natural to glance at the most popular errors and heresies upon the subject I was treating of; I might perhaps even have taken two or three of Colenso's " difficulties" by way of illustration ; but I should have dealt with these difficulties in my own way, quite independently of the form in which that writer has chosen to put them. Still less, should I have enumerated all, or provided a separate answer for each. Indeed, I should have dealt largely and principally in general and indirect arguments. And I should have relied upon these instructions as abundantly sufficient, under God, to protect my flock from the danger of corruption ; I should have considered that they had been thus provided with sufficient positive information on the one side, to counteract the effect of those mere doubts and suspicions which the public press would soon be setting before them, on the other.

But, supposing this preventive measure to have been omitted, or in this or that particular case to have failed—supposing an individual, into whose mind the poisoned shaft of doubt had already penetrated in the shape of some argument or arguments extracted from Colenso—then I should misdoubt the possibility of expelling the poison and healing the wound, merely by supplying wholesome food, or by any treatment of the general constitution of the patient ; I should feel myself bound to provide, wherever it was possible, a specific antidote to the poison imbibed, lest an uneasy suspicion should arise in the mind that the Bible had been convicted of falsehood. And from what I hear, I feel that much mischief has already been done to persons who pick up their knowledge of these things from newspapers or from conversations at the clubs, on 'change, or in the market-place (for in all these places is the subject now discussed), and do not know where to turn for a Catholic reply; and as for the Protestant replies, they are so bewildered by their number and variety, that they know not which to select, so that it often ends in their reading no answer at all. I think therefore that it may be worth while to collect for these persons a few answers to the most important of Colenso's objections, not that I have a word to say which has not been very well said, somewhere and by somebody, already, or that is not perfectly familiar to all educated Catholics who have thought on the subject at all. But the misfortune is that not all Catholics are educated, and not all educated Catholics have thought about it, whereas this book of Colenso's is in everybody's hands and everybody is talking about it.

Indeed this seems to me the special danger of this work—far beyond any authority it may receive from the ecclesiastical position of the author—that it is so eminently suited for popular use; it is " Infidelity made easy," " Infidelity for the million." Its arguments, being almost entirely arithmetical, are not above the level of the meanest capacity. He tells us himself that it was his object to put his case " in a form intelligible to the most unlearned layman," and in this he has certainly succeeded. For all Englishmen have a real practical familiarity with the first four rules of Arithmetic, but not all know much about the Bible. Consequently, many of his readers pay no attention to the conditions of the problems he proposes; very probably they are not competent to form an opinion about them, if they did; but they look only to the working of his sum, and if this is correct, they at once admit his conclusion; whereas a more accurate knowledge of the subject would often enable them to dispute and disprove the conditions under which he has stated it.

I cannot undertake to follow Colenso through every detail of his difficulties; but I should like to select fair samples of them, and give you specimens of the kind of direct answers which it seems to me they fairly admit. I shall confine myself to that which is his *specialité*, the numbers, or the time, or the space, or some other arithmetical items involved in the narrative of the Exodus. It is true indeed that he has chosen to complicate the matter in dispute by the adroit introduction of other topics; but these do not form the staple of his argument. Thus, he more than insinuates his disbelief of the miracles that are contained in the same portion of Holy Writ. He protests most loudly against being required to believe that the deluge was universal, or that the rod of Moses was changed into a living serpent, or that the waters of the Jordan ever stood in a heap, or that the sun and moon stood still, or that Balaam's ass spoke like a man; nay, so impatient is he of anything out of the ordinary course of nature, that he cannot bear that the sacred text should testify concerning the children of Israel at the Exodus, that "there was not one feeble person among their tribes." Nevertheless, he is very careful to tell us that he does not, in his present work at least, rest any of the weight of his argument upon the impossibility or improbability, either of miracles in general, or of any of these miracles in particular. He impeaches the general veracity of the record, even in matters which it narrates as facts of common history, and so undermines at once all evidence of the miracles; he says that the record contains many

" palpable contradictions and manifest impossibilities," to which he " cannot, as a true man, any longer shut his eyes." The most remarkable of these self-contradictions and impossibilities, " lying," as he says, "on the surface of the narrative," has been briefly stated as follows.

" Seventy persons going down into Egypt and remaining there 230 years could not have grown to a population of two millions, which seems to be *about* the number implied in the book of Exodus; if they had so grown, they could not have been led out of Egypt by Moses in a single day; neither could they have had tents, nor carried them, if they had ; neither could they have taken their cattle with them, nor fed them, if they had ; neither could they have had lambs enough for the Passover, nor kept the feast, if they had ; neither could they have been armed ; for if they were, they would not have been dismayed at their Egyptian pursuers ; and if they were not, how could they have fought with the Amalekites ?" Moreover, the number of the first-born is inconsistent with the number of adults and of the whole population ; the spaces of the wilderness are not extensive enough for the encampment of such hosts, nor its resources sufficient to maintain them, &c., &c., and so on, through a perfect maze of figures and arithmetical calculations *usque ad nauseam.*

Now it is with reference to such objections as these that some critics, belonging to what would be called the orthodox party among Protestants, have not hesitated to concede the palm of victory to their assailant. I have already quoted the language of one, who is of opinion that " Colenso has demonstrated a consistency in error pervading every part of the Exodus narrative;" but wishing to save the credit of the Bible, he suggests that our translators have misunderstood the Hebrew mode of numeration, and seriously proposes to divide the numbers as they at present stand, by 10, which he thinks would be a nearer approximation to the truth. Another grants that " *some* of the figures, such as the extent of population, the ratio of propagation, the proportion of the first-born to the whole mass, cannot possibly be true under the circumstances stated in Scripture." A third deprecates arithmetical criticism of the Pentateuch altogether, on the plea that *no* ancient document can stand such a test; that the history of Herodotus, for instance, is full of similar mistakes ; that if that historian gives both the items and the total of a sum, the *probability* is that they don't tally ; and why should we expect greater accuracy in the Bible History which is so much older ? A fourth goes further still, and thinks it

B

sufficient to answer, that in the same way the Waverly Novels disregard numbers, time, space, weight, &c., and yet that such inaccuracies in no way interfere with our admiration of those compositions! Even Dr. Stanley allows that there may be " *exaggerations* in the numbers;" and somebody else suggests that when once a blunder had crept in, there would be *intentional* alterations made, in order to make all harmonize.

Let these suffice by way of specimens of the extravagant license to which orthodox Protestant criticism has proceeded in order to escape from Colenso's difficulties. One is tempted to ask, If this is to be allowed in the friends and advocates of the Bible, what remains to be done by its enemies? There can be no doubt that Colenso speaks much more correctly than his critics upon this topic, when he condemns this system of arbitrary meddling with the numbers of the Pentateuch not only as rash and unauthorised, but as utterly useless for the object in view; since, as he truly says, "the number (of the population of Israel) is woven, as a kind of thread, into the whole story of the Exodus, and it cannot be taken out without tearing the whole fabric to pieces." Is it possible then to solve these difficulties in any other way? I think it is, in nine cases out of ten, and if a tenth remains an inextricable difficulty, I should be quite content to leave it so. For we cannot accept the position laid down by some of Colenso's friends, viz., "that even if some, nay the greater part of the difficulties urged by the Bishop should be proved to be untenable, yet the main result of his researches would not be materially affected; that this result is abundantly secured, if but a few points remain as incontrovertible." This I emphatically deny. The point which Colenso seeks to establish is "the unhistorical character of the Pentateuch:" and he attempts to establish this by enumerating some 20 or 30 "contradictions or impossibilities," as he calls them, in the narrative. Now I say that every such alleged contradiction, satisfactorily explained, weakens the force of those which remain; creates a presumption, that *those* too would admit of a satisfactory explanation, if only the whole circumstances of the case were known to us; and this, I think, is what must be admitted by every impartial observer of the controversy.

There is another principle also, which I think is very important to insist upon, viz., that the weight of Colenso's argument is destroyed, if, on any not violently improbable hypothesis, it can be shewn that the Scriptural statements, either of facts or numbers, are possible. For the Scriptures are (so to say) *in possession*, and it is for Colenso to dispossess them, if he can ; the *onus probandi* lies on him ; he undertakes to demonstrate the impossibility, the "absolute self-contradiction" of the Narrative ; and we hold him to his bond. If we can shew that the Scriptural statements are not impossible, we have done all that can be required of us, especially in the case of a narrative so brief and condensed as the Bible narrative is, and relating to events which happened so many thousand years ago. This principle once admitted —and I do not see how it can be fairly called in question— we are at once enabled to dispose of a certain number of Colenso's difficulties, which seem to be captious rather than critical ; and with reference to which I find it very hard to believe in the sincerity of the objector. They are capable of so obvious and natural an explanation, that to insist upon them as " contradictions" or " impossibilities," seems to argue a real desire to make mountains out of molehills.

Take, for example, his second and third difficulties, " the size of the court of the Tabernacle compared with the number of the congregation," and " Moses and Josue addressing all Israel." Holy Scripture says (Levit. viii. 3-4) that God commanded all the congregation to be gathered together at the door of the Tabernacle, and that this summons was obeyed ; whereupon Colenso pulls out his rule and measure, and proves to a demonstration that the thing is impossible. " Allowing two feet in width for each full-grown man, and eighteen inches between each rank, the adult males of the congregation alone (setting aside old men, women and children) would have reached for a distance of more than 100,000 feet—in fact, nearly twenty miles." Moreover, suppose them to have been all assembled there in any way you please, still neither Moses nor Josue could ever have read " in the ears of all the people" what they are said to have read in Deut. i. 1. Jos. viii. 34-35.

Here are two of the impossibilities which are to destroy the credibility of the Pentateuch ! Yet first, it has been well asked whether similar impossibilities could not be detected in *every* Book of History, whether ancient or modern, whose veracity however remains quite unimpeached. How often is an army said to have assembled at a village which could not have contained a tithe of its hosts ? Is not the House of Commons summoned and said to appear at the Bar of the House of Lords, in a space which could not contain a third of their number ? Dr. M'Caul has very happily quoted from

the *Moniteur* of July 16, 1790, and June 10, 1794, similar
accounts of speeches delivered and oaths taken at meetings in
the Champ de Mars, Paris, to which the whole nation had
been summoned, and which were really attended by more than
200,000 men. These answers, and such as these, turning
wholly upon the ordinary use of language, will be sufficient
to satisfy many minds as to the true value of this objection.
But secondly, it may justly be insisted upon that nothing
could be more possible or probable than that only the elders
and representatives of the people should have been summoned on these occasions. Scripture itself intimates to us
that this was really the fact (that Moses spoke to the elders,
and the elders to the people) in other cases, where the
letter of the Sacred Text would seem at first to have stated
that Moses himself communicated directly with the people.
Compare Exod. iv. 29-31, xii. 3, with xii. 21, xix. 3, 7, 8,
xxxiv. 30-32.

Let us pass on to the next impossibility in Colenso's for-
midable catalogue. The camp was (perhaps) twelve miles
square, and the tabernacle was in the middle of it; how then
could the priests have carried on their backs for six miles to
the outside of the camp the whole carcase of a bullock, with
its skin, entrails, and the rest, as the law required them to
do? See Levit. iv. 11, 12. I would answer, your mode of
literal interpretation is as opposed to common sense as it is
to the genius of the Scriptural language. If it were admitted, we should be obliged to believe that Moses was a
mason or a carpenter because God said to him, "*Thou shalt
make* an altar" (Exod. xxx. 1)—and a goldsmith; "thou shalt
overlay it with the purest gold" (ibid. v. 3)—and a tailor;
" Thou shalt make a holy vesture for Aaron; moreover for the
sons of Aaron thou shalt prepare linen tunics." (xxviii. 2, 40.)
We must believe also that Pilate personally inflicted the cruel
scourging upon our Lord, because the words of St. Matthew
(xxvii. 26) literally say so. It has been well suggested that
Holy Scripture speaks of "waggons for the service of the
Tabernacle," (Numbers vii. 3, 6,) and has Colenso satisfied
himself that this was not one of the uses to which those
waggons were put? Lastly, and above all, can he deny what
all Hebrew scholars insist upon, that the word used in the
original directly excludes his interpretation, and can only
properly be translated as signifying that "the priest should
CAUSE *to be carried out*"?*

* If any one still doubts this solution of the *difficulty*, let him refer to Leviticus
xvi 27, 28, where the pronouns used seem *necessarily* to imply that some one else,
not the priest, carried forth the sacrifice without the camp.

The fifth of Colenso's difficulties appears at first sight perhaps of a more serious character than those which I have already examined; yet on closer inspection it will not, I think, prove very difficult to deal with. It is briefly this; that the law contains a general command that whenever a numbering of the people shall take place, a certain poll-tax should be paid towards the maintenance of the sanctuary (Exod. xxx. 11-13). By and bye (xxxviii. 25) we read of such a tribute having been collected, but without any mention of a census having been taken, (I quote from Colenso; but any one consulting the Bible for himself will probably think otherwise,) and *rice versa*, a few months later still, we read of a census, but without any mention of the tribute (Numbers i. 1-46.) Colenso allows that the omission in each case might be considered as accidental, one part of an action being in both instances put for the whole; but he calls our attention to a circumstance which he qualifies as surprising, viz. that the number of adult males was identically the same on the first occasion as it was half a year afterwards. It would be surprising indeed, if this were quite such a self-contradiction in the narrative as Colenso supposes. I mean, it is *too* palpable to have been an oversight in any forger, or interpolator, of the history. Any honest man, reading the two statements and not wishing to "make out a case" against the writer, would say at once that there was probably but one numbering of the people for both purposes; that even if it be certain (which it is not) that there were six months between the two events as recorded in Scripture, yet that the same returns may have been made use of for the two purposes, which (as we have seen) were in fact, by the very letter of the law, so intimately united. Both the enrolment and the payment of the tribute concerned the males among the children of Israel " from twenty years old and upwards;" neither of them could have been completed in a single day : yet some fixed point would certainly have been taken from which the attainment of majority was to be reckoned for all. Is there anything improbable in the conjecture which has been made, that this point may have been "the first day of the first month," the day on which the "tabernacle was set up" (Exodus xl. 2.) for which this tribute was required? On this hypothesis, the tribute might have been paid prospectively in some instances ; i.e. there would have been some who would not have attained their majority at the very moment it was paid, yet might have been required to pay notwithstanding, because they would be of age on or before the day which had been

fixed as the standard, the day on which the tabernacle was
set up : and contrariwise, there would have been others who
would have attained their majority during the month that
intervened between the setting up of the tabernacle and the
numbering of the people, yet whose names would not appear
in the census, for the same reason ; viz. because they were
not of age on the first day of the new year which had been
chosen as the starting point ; and so the numbers might have
been identical, even if there were two distinct numberings of
the people at two separate times. This, however, I do not
myself believe ; the very words of Scripture, when speaking
of the tax (Exod. xxxviii. 25), that the money "was offered
by *them that went to be numbered*," seem to me clearly to
point to the future census ; to show that the census was the
principal thing, to which the offering was only an accessory.
In other words, I see no reason for believing that the offer-
ings here spoken of were made at any other time than at the
taking of the census, and I suppose them to be inserted here
by anticipation, in order to complete the subject in hand, by
naming the cost of all those things which had just been so
fully described. However, be this as it may, all I am concerned to shew is, that, even if there were two numberings,
at an interval of a few months, the identity of the numbers
might on some hypothesis be accounted for. It is not an
impossibility. I am well aware that even so, there will still
remain enough for a captious critic to cavil at, since, according to the ordinary laws of nature, there must have been
some deaths among so large a number in the course of the
intervening months, however few they may have been. But
this is a difficulty which I think we can afford to pass over,
as St. Austin passed over other difficulties proposed by persons whom he characterises as *otiosi et scrupulosi, paratiores
ad interrogandum quàm capaciores ad intelligendum.** Or,
if we *must* give a direct answer, what is to prevent our adopt-
ing another hypothesis altogether, and supposing that by a
wonderful coincidence the number of deaths during these
months exactly equalled the number of those who attained
their majority during the same period ?

Let us approach his sixth *Enstasis*. He quotes Exodus
xvi. 16, where the people are commanded to gather a certain

* De Civ. Dei. xv. 1. Other chapters of this book might be usefully studied by
persons, really perplexed by Colenso's arithmetical difficulties ; e.g. c. 13, where he
accounts for frequent errors in the transcription of numbers, because they don't
arrest and fix the attention, where there is nothing difficult to understand or useful
to learn. *Quis enim existimet sibi esse discendum, quot millia hominum tribus Israel
singillatim habere potuerunt, quoniam prodesse aliquid non putatur, &c.*

measure of manna for every man, " according to the number of your souls that dwell in a *tent*." It is this last word which destroys the historical credibility of the Pentateuch ! How could the Israelites have had *anything* so cumbrous as tents, so soon after their hasty flight out of Egypt ? Were they of canvas, or of skins ? and how large were they? and how were they carried ? One ox perhaps might have carried one tent, with all its apparatus of pegs and poles and cords ; but then oxen won't carry goods, unless they have been trained ; and how could the Israelites have trained them ? This is the way in which Colenso heaps question upon question through three successive pages ; and yet he is obliged to confess at the very outset that it would seem clear from Levit. xxiii. 42, 43, that the people dwelt in *booths* in the wilderness, i.e. in rough temporary tents (so to call them) made out of the boughs of trees. But then booths are not tents, and tents are not booths ; and though the words are sometimes in the Bible interchanged "improperly" (so says Colenso himself), yet it *shall* not be so here ; in this passage (Exodus xvi. 16) and all other similar passages, tents *shall* mean real and proper tents, made *secundum artem :* and then I'll prove the Bible History to be false, because the Israelites could not possibly have had such tents. Was ever more miserable petty special pleading heard in disputes between man and man ? and this is the critical method of an "honest enquirer after truth," practised upon the Bible, which he has always professed to receive and reverence as the Word of God !

Nor is his mode of dealing with the next " difficulty" very different. " The children of Israel went up *armed* out of the land of Egypt" (Exod. xiii. 18). How could this be ? would the Egyptians have allowed it ? or, if it was, how came the Israelites to be afraid when they found the Egyptians were pursuing them (xiv. 10) ? Surely this is a " self-contradiction." Yet is there anything to cause even a moment's surprise in the panic of a " mixed multitude" (xii. 38) of men, women, and children, escaping in haste from a country where they had been so long oppressed and trodden down, and now encumbered with their herds, flocks, and all they possessed, and pursued by a numerous and well-trained army of their enemies, their late masters ? Or is there anything difficult in supposing that *some* of the Israelites were armed, though others were not? Or rather, *must* not some of them have been men of wealth and substance, and consequently been in possession of arms? How else could the Egyptians have been afraid of them, and said " they are *stronger* than we ?"

(Exod. i. 9). Again, is it quite certain that the word really means "armed?" For we are told that it is a word of very rare occurrence and doubtful etymology; some persons would have it translated, "in companies of fifty;" others "in military array;" others again, "equipped," or furnished with all things necessary for their journey. But because the word "armed" might create a difficulty, therefore Colenso prefers this and insists upon it.

We have seen enough to justify us in saying that this is a *characteristic* of his mode of argument. Where there are two ways of understanding a passage, this critic invariably prefers that which creates, or magnifies, a difficulty. We have a striking instance in his very next chapter. He *will* have it that the instruction how to keep the Passover was given only on the very day on which it was actually to be kept, so that it could not possibly have been communicated to so large a multitude within the proper time. Look at Exodus xii. 3, 6, 12, for yourself, and see what you think about this difficulty. If you consult the Vulgate or the Douay translation, I am sure you will marvel where the difficulty lies, how such a notion ever could have entered any body's head. If however you study closely either the Hebrew or the authorised Protestant translation, you will see the little word which has proved the stumbling-block to our enquirer. Even in these versions, verses 3 and 6 would seem to make it clear, that the injunctions about the Passover were given on the tenth day of the month at least, if not earlier; but when you read in verse 12 "*this*" day (instead of *that*), you may begin to doubt. One or other of the verses must be made to bend *somewhat*, to bring them to perfect apparent harmony; which shall we meddle with? Suppose that little word "this" to have been used prospectively; that is to say, suppose the speaker so thoroughly to have identified himself with the subject and the day of which he is speaking, that he thinks and speaks of it as though it were already present—and examples are not wanting both in Hebrew and English to warrant such a use of the word—see verses 14 and 17 of this same chapter—and the difficulty vanishes at once; insist upon the ordinary strictest sense of the word "this," as denoting the day *on* which, not *of* which the speaker is discoursing, and the whole passage becomes perplexing and self-contradictory: of course Colenso accepts the latter alternative.

In connection with this same point, of haste and suddenness in the Exodus, much stress is laid on the impossility of the Israelites "borrowing" of the Egyptians so much silver and gold and raiment as the Bible speaks of, under such circumstances. But there are not wanting passages in the narrative which seem to prove that an intimation of this borrowing had been given to Moses from the first (Exod. iii. 22); that it had been repeated, and probably in some measure acted upon, that is to say, the Israelites had probably made the demand, either on the plea of wages for unrequited labour, or compensation for the immoveable property they were going to leave behind them, before the last plague (xi. 2), but it was only consented to at last by the Egyptians, under the influence of the panic occasioned by the death of the first-born. (xii. 35.)

Nor is this the only instance in which Colenso has been guilty of great carelessness, if not of something worse, in his mode of dealing with the Sacred text. See how he urges the impossibility of so many Israelites with their flocks and herds living so long in such a dry and barren wilderness; how pertinaciously he insists upon this want of water, which he says was not always or often miraculously supplied, "for the rock did not follow them, as some have supposed;" and one of the texts amongst others which he quotes to support his thesis is this; "I was thy leader in the great and terrible wilderness, wherein there was the serpent burning with his breath, *and no waters at all.*" These words he *Italicizes,* as I have done, as God's own description of the wilderness; and there he stops. The very next words of the text are these, " who *brought forth streams out of the hardest rock,* and fed thee in the wilderness with Manna which thy fathers knew not." (Deut. viii. 15). Why were these words omitted? Do they not, in their true connection, obviously suggest the very opposite to what Colenso wished to prove? Is it not as though God would remind those to whom He spoke, of the *natural* drought and desolation in the wilderness through which He had brought them, and at the same time of the *supernatural* plenty with which His goodness never failed to supply them? Finally, is not this also what we should have naturally inferred from the expression in St. Paul's Epistle to the Corinthians, (I. x. 4), " the Spiritual *rock that followed them.*"

One more instance of our author's carelessness, or want of good faith, and I have done with this part of my subject. Assuming without any express warrant of Holy Scripture,— if I ought not rather to say, contrary to the plain statement of Scripture; certainly contrary to the opinion of some of the most learned commentators—that all the laws about sacrifices, and other ceremonial observances, were faithfully kept during the wanderings in the wilderness, he objects that each of the three priests (Aaron and his two sons, Nadab and Abiu, being now dead) would have had to eat for his *daily* portion about eighty-eight pigeons, besides the shoulders and breasts of oxen or of sheep that may have been offered in sacrifice, &c. ; whereas it is distinctly written, "the priests *and Levites, and all that are of the same tribe* [of Levi]...... *shall eat* the sacrifices of the Lord and His oblations." (Deut. xviii. 1.) Compare Numbers, iii. 6, viii. 19, 24.

I have now gone through more than half of Colenso's difficulties and contradictions, taking them in his own order of arrangement (excepting that, for the present, I have omitted the first, which is of a somewhat different character,) and I think you will agree with the judgment I passed on them at the beginning, viz. : that many of them are captious rather than critical, and betray a manifest desire to make mountains out of mole-hills. Nobody can believe that these were the difficulties which *first* roused the author's doubts as to the credibility of the Mosaic narrative ; nor can any scholar give him credit for having really examined them with sufficient care, or with an unbiassed judgment. But this is not what you or I are immediately concerned with ; we only care for the effect which the difficulties themselves may have on the minds of any Catholics to whose knowledge they may be brought ; and I confess I cannot apprehend serious evil from such as these to an honest and good heart. No doubt, they may furnish ready weapons to a man already disbelieving, or wishing to disbelieve, the whole Gospel scheme, and who is therefore on the look out for some excuse to justify his unbelief both to himself and others ; and for this reason, it is well to be prepared with some solution of them ; but in themselves, I repeat that I do not think they are capable of doing serious mischief. Some of the other difficulties however which yet remain are of a graver kind ; and of these I will write another day. Meanwhile, let me hear what you think of my answers to these ; they do not pretend to be anything learned or original, but simply to be useful and sufficient. Let me hear also more in detail the kind of answer you would propose to adopt.

Si quid novisti rectius istis,
Candidus imperti ; si non his utere mecum.

Yours ever affectionately,

S. N.

LETTER III.

Dear Doctor,

I am sincerely obliged to you for the trouble you have taken in answering my letter. But, if it be modest to say so, I like my own way best after all. *Chacun à son goût!* You are a man of facts and figures, while I feel myself more at home in dealing with *principles*. I think I recollect that you, or one of your friends, once compiled an index to Herodotus, carefully noting every individual fact which that gossiping historian has recorded ; as, for example, who was the tallest man in Greece, who the handsomest; what was the length and breadth of a sheep's tail in Arabia, what the height of the pyramids in Egypt, &c., &c. The very thought of such an undertaking as this is enough to give one a headache. There are no doubt phases of the human mind and character which your treatment would suit rather than mine, but you would find it, I venture to say, in the vast majority of cases, a wearisome and unprofitable task. Besides, when all is done, when you have answered to your satisfaction each one of Colenso's objections, what have you gained ? You have set the inquirer's mind at rest for the time being; but that is all. You have not cured him ; your method does not pretend to grapple with the enemy in the fortress of his power; it is merely a system of skirmishing. For a person who really believed at heart, but whose fancy was haunted and his reason perplexed with difficulties, your arguments might suffice ; but for one who was really wanting *in faith*, and not merely troubled and puzzled, you only provide a temporary relief. His old doubts and difficulties would recur, or fresh objections be started about matters not met in your answers. Objections may be multiplied *ad infinitum :* what have you gained by answering any number of them ? The publication of some mischievous book, a glance at some sceptical article in a review, a paragraph in a newspaper, a random remark of some unbelieving acquaintance, would upset the work you had finished, or thought you had finished, with such infinite pains. Then, again, you are satisfied, no doubt, with your own performance, and you have good reason to be so. Far be it from me to underrate your work. But as you tell me in your letter that my method is incomplete without yours, I may answer that much more so is yours without mine. These answers, then, which to your mind seem so convincing, will they—are you quite certain—appear equally convincing to the minds of others? Remember how variously different men's minds are affected by reasonings; by the reasonings, for instance, of commentators on the Classical Authors. Will he who consults you put more faith in your comments on Moses, than you yourself put in Bentley upon Horace, or Johnson upon Shakespeare, or Lombardi upon Dante? If so, *he has faith already;* he regards you as one having authority to teach and distinguish what is matter of faith from what is matter of opinion. He is only some weakminded Catholic who has been tempted, not convinced by Colenso. But how about the poor unbeliever who is making his religion out of his own head? How about the poor Protestant who is consciously, or unconsciously, doing the very same thing? These, I repeat, are merely put off with an answer which appears (if it really appears so) sufficient for the time being. They never had any faith before consulting you: they have none after having consulted you; nor are they even on the road towards it.

But you ask me to give some fuller description of the sort of indirect treatment which I recommend. I will do so.

I would ask the inquirer, in the first place, this simple question—whether religion be a Divine or a human thing? whether (that is to say) God Himself has taught us what we are to believe and do in order to please Him, or whether He has left each man to settle this matter of his own wit or fancy? He will probably answer, that he has undertaken the search after Truth, with no other guide than that light of reason which God has implanted in his breast—save that as he is only a weak and fallible man, he trusts that God Himself will be his guide in the use of it, and that He will bring him finally to the knowledge of the Truth. This statement of the case, though at first sight it seems very plausible, involves consequences of the most astounding nature when considered in detail, which I should now proceed to put before him. God Himself forbid, I would rejoin, that I should disparage His greatest earthly gift. And surely we may abuse it; we may allot it a work for which it was never designed, to which it is naturally unequal; and, in that case, vainly shall we expect the Divine co-operation. And do you really believe, that the Almighty has set you to this most laborious, and superhuman task of making a religion for yourself? This would be to say, that He means and requires of you to examine the claims of Mahometanism, Buddhism, Catholicism, and the various sects of Protestantism; that you have to consider the evidences, external and internal, of these opposite forms of religion; that you study and compare together the Koran, the Zendavesta, and the Bible; that you discuss, on the one hand, the abstruse question of the possibility of miracles, and then go on to weigh critically the evidences for their actual occurrence; that you invent or discover canons for the purpose of discerning true from false miracles; that supposing you are chiefly attracted towards the Bible, yet, as it can help you in nothing towards the grand object of inquiry, unless you shall be fully convinced that it is the word of God, you go into the question of its inspiration. Here you must either suppose that there is a savour (so to speak) about an inspired work which proves at once that it is inspired, and that upon hearing quoted a passage from Shakespeare, from the Koran, a proverb of King Solomon, a sentiment from some classical author, you shall by the said savour detect the inspired from the uninspired passage (which can hardly be maintained by any one), or you must suppose on the other hand that there is no such savour about the inspired writings—no *a priori* notion of inspiration; and then you must take Jowett's notion *that inspiration is that idea of the Bible which one gets from reading the Bible*, and that so far from viewing the Bible beforehand as a Sacred Book, we ought to start with treating it as a profane book, and subject it to the same laws of criticism as any other book : and then, if there be anything in which it is unlike any other book—any savour of Divine Inspiration—that will disengage itself and be evolved in the process. Here, then, you will have to consider the Bible narrative as compared with other histories sacred and profane. The ancient and sacred books of most nations start with a *Theogony* and *Cosmogony*. Moses must be compared with other writers of this class : his narrative of the foundation of the world must be also compared with the investigations of scientific men. The various theories and discoveries of these must be studied in their turn. Then the history of Moses must be compared part with part, and the difficulties and objections of such writers as Voltaire, Colenso, and others, be fairly dealt with. The moral teaching of the Sacred Books must form a separate subject of investigation. Whether these overwhelming and anxious labours will have resulted, at last, in the conclusion that the Bible is the Word of God, is, to say the least, very questionable. Rather, a logical mind which started with viewing it as a human book would go on to explain it throughout in a human way, and find nothing but a human element in it. Prophecy would be reduced to mere poetry; miracles would be convulsions of nature, or else fables; the "Word of the Lord," an inward prompting of the heart; and thus the supernatural altogether eliminated. But supposing on the other hand you be not over logical, and conclude that the Bible is, according to the common understanding of the expression, the Word of God; yet it has further to be considered that the Bible is not really one book, but a collection of many books, written at various times and by various authors; that questions have arisen at various times and amongst various religious bodies as to which of these books are inspired, and which uninspired. This will form another separate subject of inquiry. Suppose that the result of your inquiry shall be unfavourable to the books of the Old Testament, then the New Testament goes along with it. This must be so clear to every careful reader that the subject need hardly be dwelt upon. Anyhow, the New Testament has to be submitted to the same critical tests as you will have already subjected the Old, viz., to those canons of criticism which you would apply to any profane writer. Supposing, again, that your study of the New Testament shall have convinced you that Christ was truly the Son of God, you will have now to study the claims of the various Christian sects and Churches which profess to continue upon earth His Divine mission and teaching. Suppose, however, you reject the doctrine that He was God, you will hardly (if you wish to be consistent) take up with the Unitarian notion that He was merely the Model Man, divinely commissioned to teach authoritatively those sublime truths of the *Unity of God* and *the Immortality of the Soul*, which had been previously held as speculations. For either surely He was what the Jews would have stoned Him for declaring Himself; or He was what reverence forbids me to say. You will now have attached yourself to some one Christian Church or sect; *which one* I cannot venture to say, save that you cannot have become a Catholic; for this would involve giving up the principle which you started with, and to which I must suppose you have adhered, viz., that "you follow no other guide than that light of reason which God has implanted in your breast, and God's guidance in the use of it." But you are not safe yet. The teacher you have chosen does not claim to be an infallible one: he would be shocked, he would be indignant, he would scout the notion most contemptuously; but he points to *the Book.* That at any rate is the Word of God, who is Infallible, who is the very Truth. And then comes the question, whether you yourself may not have erred. Is it

after all the Word of God ? Was there no false step at one
of the many turnings in the painful inquiry ?—" Will not
some day, or other, a discovery be made, or some flaw in the
train of reasoning be brought to light by others, or occur to
myself, which will overset the whole structure ? There is
certainly this great thought to support me, that I am under
the guidance of God" (you will say), " but how then with so
many thousand others who have taken the same pains, yet
have come to infinitely various conclusions ; are they all in-
sincere ? am I alone in earnest ? Then, again, though the
Bible be the Word of God, yet how variously it is interpreted
by its readers. It is undeniably a fruitful source of sects and
schisms. The Roman Catholics have one interpretation, Protestants another, the German Rationalists and their representatives another. Each sect of Protestantism has its favourite
passages which seem to countenance the peculiarity or practice
belonging to the sect; nay, each man has his own religion.
Am I alone right, I alone under the Divine Guidance, I alone
in earnest ?"

I will not suppose you to remain a Protestant, for, as a
rule, no sincere enquirer can do so. One must stifle inquiry ;
one must give over thinking out of very weariness; one must
suppose (though against the plain letter and spirit of Scripture) that God cares nothing about what a man believes so that
he do that which is right ; one must resign oneself to doubts
and difficulties and inconsistencies of doctrine, as the
natural order of things, as a part of our earthly probation ;
one must turn from the very thought of religious controversy
as from a painful subject. This do, and you may remain a
Protestant. Distract your attention from the bitter realities
around you : throw yourself heart and soul into your profes-
sion, or business : exercise yourself in works of charity and
benevolence : compound for the exercise of the intellect by
the exercise of the heart and affections ;—and you may still
remain a Protestant. Do anything but *think* about matters
of doctrine. But you are lost as a Protestant, if you indulge
the taste for inquiry. Do you not know that to a logical
mind inconsistency is the sin of sins ? Yet this is the very
first direction your mind will take : it will want to be rid of
inconsistencies ; and in this desire you will take one of two
roads : Germany or Rome must be your goal. The fact is
patent. How can you believe that God cares nothing about
what you believe, and believe the Bible to be the Word
of God, which anathematises the unbeliever, be he man or
even " an angel from heaven ?" How can you claim the

right of following no other guide than the light of reason within you, and God's guidance in the use of it, and yet protest against one whose reasonings lead him to the conclusion, that it is the most reasonable act to submit one's reason to God speaking through His Church? How can you claim to be guided by the light of reason in the face of the plain statement, " If he will not hear the Church, let him be to thee as a heathen or a publican?" How can you accept the word of God that "the gates of Hell shall never prevail against his Church," and put up with the fact of the bewildering confusion of creeds and sects in Protestantism? No: if you should ever be a Protestant you will not continue a Protestant, and continue to think earnestly about doctrinal matters. But you will either follow the path which leads to Rome though it involves the surrender of your principle; or you will follow the Rationalists, and then indeed you will have free scope to follow out your principle. You will be guided by reason and by reason alone, and that which is unintelligible will be considered unreasonable. At the start you may be a Deist; you will accept the Bible only so far as it coincides with Reason, and Nature. You will profess a system of Natural Religion, a "Religion of the Reason," without an altar, without sacraments, without any special religious ordinances of any kind whatsoever—a Religion of *savans*, which never took hold of the populace; this for a time, perhaps, will be your religion. The masses, I say, will not care much for you or your religion. *They* want some token to the eye, and the ear, and the touch. They would sooner turn to fetish-worship itself than embrace your system which they would not even comprehend. You will not, meantime, remain stationary, save by the surrender of thinking. You will find, in your German books, a statement that will, at first, startle you; but from frequent repetition you will get accustomed to it. It is this, that the Christian Dogma of Creation out of nothing is inconceivable or contradictory. Then there is nothing for it, but the identification of the universe with the Deity. You are now a Pantheist, or Atheist, for it is all one ; the former term is only a finer word than the latter to express the same idea. You are an Atheist, but you cannot complain : you are where your first principle has fairly landed you. The doctrine that creation out of nothing is inconceivable or contradictory, is accounted by rationalistic writers as a mere truism, which it is not worth while proving. It is needless to reply that though this doctrine may seem contradictory to our minds, yet it may not be contradictory in itself; that it is above reason, perhaps, but not therefore unreasonable. This is well enough for one who takes the ground of authority; but for one who like yourself has undertaken to make a religion of the reason, that must evidently be rejected which does not approve itself as such, reasonable. You are an Atheist, really, though you may still call yourself a Protestant if you choose, with as much reason as some of the writers of Essays and Reviews. But enough.

Where has been the Divine guidance all this while? Where do you see in the Babel of creeds, and the contrary winds of doctrine which war against each other, in this as in any other Protestant country any token of Divine Guidance? No: God does not, will not guide those who make a religion out of their own heads either with or without the Bible. Reason was, clearly, not given us to construct a Religious System, but to discover the Teaching Authority. Why do you come to me with Colenso's difficulties? What is this, but beginning altogether at the wrong end? That Faith is necessary for salvation is equally the dictum of Revelation and Common Sense—the belief that God Himself must teach us what we are to believe and do in order to the salvation of our souls. The only faith you have had all this time has been a false faith, as the result clearly shows; a belief that God would guide you in doing what He never intended you to do. For the rest, you have had faith in nothing but yourself; and you have reaped the consequences of your own self-sufficiency. You have never known, you will never know (on your own principle) what it is to rest in the full assurance of God's guidance. He only who believes *in God*, finds rest for his mind and reason.

"And does God teach men Himself?" you will ask. This would be a boon indeed!—O! believe it, that He does! There is one Church, maligned and blackened and misrepresented, whose very name is evil in the mouths of her enemies, whose destruction these enemies are always plotting, whose fall they have, time out of mind, been prophesying, yet behold! she lives and promises to live. Unlike those noisy sects which do not claim to be infallible, she both claims to be God's Mouth-Piece, and will support her claim by those signs which common-sense teaches such a claimant ought to manifest. She is one and the same in all the four quarters of the world. She is not the religion of a race or a nation, but embraces within her fold men of every clime, of every race and station, barbarian and civilized, rich and poor. She has survived the

c

various revolutions which have swept over the nations since her establishment. She embraces those truths in one synthesis which other religions exhibit fragmentarily.* She has been illustrious in Saints throughout the ages; she can exhibit her pedigree and title-deeds, back to the first ages when they who founded her amongst the nations sealed their witness with their life's blood. I do not ask you to believe this on my bare statement. I only ask you to examine for yourself, and to hear her own account about herself, and not to accept without examination the statements of her enemies. Anyhow it is premature to study Colenso's difficulties, before you know even that you will be required to answer them. But if I have brought you to admit that God Himself must be our Teacher, the first question surely is, to find out *where, how*, and *to whom* He speaks : all else is of the most secondary importance. At the day of reckoning you will not be required to render account as to whether or not you have carefully and conscientiously studied Colenso ; but if God has spoken, you will indeed have to answer as to why you have not heard His voice. If He has set up His Church amongst the nations, you will indeed have to answer as to wherefore you have not been a member of it, and wherefore you have presumed to make a religion out of your own head. But when once you have listened to the voice of God, when you have found Him and know that it is He who speaks and not another, then you will make little account (if you be faithful) of what man shall devise and declare in opposition to Him. Perplexed you may be, tempted you may be, for faith must have its probation like every other virtue ; but your feet will rest firm on the Rock of His strength, and your heart will neither be moved nor troubled. Until you have considered this all-important matter, it will be superfluous to treat of Colenso's objections. Any answer which you or I might devise will bring you no nearer to that Faith in God which is required of you. Rather, the more satisfactorily you answer him, the more will you be self-satisfied, and self-sufficient; while, on the other hand, when you have heard the voice of God, it will matter little whether you can answer Colenso or no. It

* "I am embracing that creed..which upholds the divinity of tradition with Laud, consent of Fathers with Beveridge, a visible Church with Bramhall, a tribunal of dogmatic decisions with Bull, the authority of the Pope with Thorndike, penance with Taylor, prayers for the dead with Ussher, celibacy, asceticism, ecclesiastical discipline with Bingham. I seek a Church which in these, and a multitude of other points, is nearer the Apostolic Church than any existing one ; which is the continuation of the Apostolic Church, if it has been continued at all." *Loss and Gain.*

will be time enough, then for me to take an interest in your enquiry; and I will engage to show that there are no greater difficulties in Religion than in Nature, and none in Colenso which cannot be paralleled in common history and common life.

Thus, my dear Doctor, would I deal with my imaginary unbeliever. I fear that long since you have been impatiently longing for the conclusion of this prosy epistle; and indeed I am wearied of it myself. But I deem it a matter of the highest importance in the present controversy, not to lose sight of our true position as Catholics, and the true position of Protestants as such. Do not think, once more, that I do not appreciate your argument, because I consider it subordinate to my own. On the contrary, I beg of you to continue it, as it will be most useful to me. I only mean that its chief usefulness will appear when my own argument (if it be successful in my hands) shall have done its work. One portion of your letter I especially appreciate, which distinguishes the real difficulties urged in Dr. Colenso's book, from those frivolous, captious objections with which they are mingled. These latter seem to convict the writer of *bad faith*.

I remain,

Respectfully and affectionately

Yours,

C. M.

LETTER IV.

My dear friend,

You and I are moving along, if not on parallel lines that will never meet, yet on roads that approach the fortress we aim at from different sides. And you travel much faster than I can, for you choose your own road, and go straight ahead, whereas the path that I have been forced into is no road at all, but a mere mass of bricks and stones and rubbish of every kind, heaped together by the enemy for the express purpose of debarring all passage. Certainly you have the advantage of me, and you know how to make the most of it. Nevertheless, mine is a humble and laborious work that *somebody* must do; and a priest has no right to refuse any work, however tedious, which may be of use for the saving of souls.

Of course, I thoroughly agree with you in considering that all attempts to answer Colenso are out of place, and would be quite unprofitable, in dealing with an unbeliever. Even with a Catholic, whose faith had been *seriously injured* by mixing with unbelievers or studying their works, I would not enter upon such a course of argument. I would insist upon his beginning with some larger, broader view of the subject, or I would not consent to argue with him at all. I would say to him what Father Newman said of me nearly twenty years ago, when he heard that I was likely to embrace the Catholic Faith, but fancied that I was entangling myself in the examination of particular historical difficulties. "When we have lost our way," he said, "we mount up to some eminence to look about us, but N. plunges into the nearest thicket to find out his bearings." Other observations in the same letter are so much to our present purpose that I cannot help copying them, and you will be pleased at seeing how exactly they coincide with some of your own remarks. He writes thus, "I am far from denying that a strong case of apparent exception to the infallibility of the Church is not sufficient to make a person pause; but to *begin* with particular cases is to begin at the wrong end.......In a very large system you necessarily must have great apparent anomalies—*as in Scripture (a parallel which might be effectively worked out)*—and you must begin by expecting these and making allowance for them. Some things, perhaps, must ever be difficulties (*as there are insoluble difficulties in Scripture*), but on the whole and in proportion as persons come *nearer* to the system, there is a growing evidence of consistency. Is it possible that a sensible man can consent to make his own mind the measure, the arbiter of perfect consistency? Will not one person be able to solve things more fully than another? Is every one therefore to stand on different ground, according to their respective success in making all things consistent? or rather, must there not be some *general* ground which all may stand upon? And this, I think, is furnished by the question of evidence, which all inquirers may have, for the consistency of the Catholic system and history."

We have but to change the word Catholic in this last sentence to Scriptural, and I think we have an argument very pertinent to the present difficulties. Indeed, you see the writer distinctly contemplated its application to objections urged against Scripture, as well as to those urged against the Church ; and if the line of argument which *you* propose for controversy with unbelievers is not strictly on the question of evidence, yet it is of the same wide and general character.

There is one point in your reasoning which I should have liked to have seen more fully developed, viz., the inviolable connection of the Old and New Testaments. You take it for granted that they must stand or fall together ; and to you or me this assumption may seem perfectly just. But I think there are several ill-instructed persons at the present moment, both Catholics and Protestants, who fondly imagine that they can save the New Testament at the expense of the Old. Surely such persons must be strangely ignorant of the true state of the case. They can never have considered how habitually Christ and His Apostles *assumed* the authority of the Jewish Scriptures throughout all their teaching ; and there is no question whatever but that we have the same Scriptures now as they had then. "Moses and the Prophets," (St. Luke xxiv. 27) "the whole law and the prophets," (St. Matt. xxii. 40.) are continually appealed to as a Divine authority by our Lord, so that He does not hesitate to say to the unbelieving Jews, "If you believed Moses, you would perhaps believe Me also, for he wrote of Me. But if you do not believe his writings, how will you believe My words ?" (St. John v. 46-7.) The weapons with which, for our sakes, He vouchsafed to combat and overcome Satan tempting Him in the wilderness were all taken from the Old Testament; two of them from this very portion of it which we are now invited to ridicule as full of contradictions and impossibilities. The "story," as Colenso would call it, of Noe and the deluge, of Lot's wife, of the burning bush, of the brazen serpent, of the manna from heaven—all these taken from the Pentateuch, are distinctly referred to by our Redeemer Himself. In addition to these, His Apostle, St. Paul, recognizes from the same source the passage through the Red Sea, the miraculous supply of water from the rock, the worship of the golden calf, the fornication of the children of Israel with the daughters of Moab, the interviews of Abraham with Melchisedec, the "stories" of Cain and Abel, Henoch, Noe, Sara, Joseph, the fall of the walls of Jericho, &c., &c. And yet these are the books which, on the strength of Colenso's figures, we are called upon to abandon as historically false, to submit to the "solvent" action of sceptical criticism and so to relegate to the region of myths; and, as I have said, there are those who dream that they can safely do this and still retain faith in Christ. Let

them not deceive themselves. Christ is " He of whom Moses
and the Prophets wrote ;" but if Colenso be true, what value
remains to the testimony of Moses ? The New Testament is
as it were the development and fulfilment of the Old ; and the
germ of both is to be found in the Books of Genesis and
Exodus; take away these, and the rest of the Bible becomes
a riddle. It has been well said that those books are " un-
mistakeably endorsed, as well by the whole subsequent
history of the Jewish nation, as by the writers of the
New Testament." It is true that Colenso only professes to
reject the *history* of the Pentateuch, but its theology must
fall with its history; they are inextricably interwoven with
one another ; and moreover, it is to the *history* of the Pentateuch, even in some of its minutest details, rather than to
any other part, that we have the most abundant Apostolic testimony. See St. Paul's first Epistle to the Corinthians,
chapter x : 2 Cor. iii. 13, &c. and the Epistle to the He-
brews *passim*. Indeed, I would beg those who think they can
divorce the two Testaments, or at least separate the Pentateuch from the rest of the Bible, to look into any concordance
of the Sacred Volume, and search out for themselves all the
words of Christ, His Prophets or Apostles, which bear witness
to the principal personages or events of the Mosaic narrative.
Then they will begin to understand what they are about ; they
will see the unavoidable issue of the path on which they
have entered. We have been lately told (Stanley's Lectures
on Jewish Church p. xiii.) that five and twenty years ago
Arnold expressed a hope that some one would arise to do for
the Jewish History what Wolf and Niebuhr had done for the
Grecian and Roman. The Books of Moses were to be han-
dled as the books of Livy or of Homer had been. In Colenso
we have a specimen of the process and the result ; and many
Protestants staggered by it, and feeling that the letter of
the Bible is the very foundation of their faith, will, it is to
be feared, be carried away by his criticisms into the dreary
waste of unbelief.

It may be easy to draw a distinction on paper,* and to say
that " it has long been the doctrine of the educated laity that
the word of God is *in* the Bible, to the utter rejection of the
notion that every word *of* the Bible has that character."
But let this principle be once consciously admitted in practice,
and what standpoint has Protestantism left ? If the word of
God is in the Bible, but not all that is in the Bible is the

'word of God, what rule have they whereby to distinguish the one part from the other? We Catholics indeed have never professed to draw our religion from the Bible; we believe in one Holy Catholic Apostolic Church, the divinely appointed teacher, "the pillar and ground of the truth." Yet, since we have always been taught to reverence the Bible as the work of men inspired by the Holy Ghost, as the written word of God, it cannot be a matter of indifference to us to hear it held up to ridicule as full of historical contradictions and impossibilities. And when these impossibilities are specified, and are of such a character as even the ignorant can appreciate, as for instance that the numbers in the book of Exodus require us to suppose that every Israelitish woman became the mother of eighty or ninety children, that at the Passover in the wilderness each priest had to kill 1250 lambs in every minute of two consecutive hours, that each priest had to consume for his own daily portion eighty or ninety pigeons, &c., &c., some from among the less educated portion of our flocks may be sorely perplexed, unless they are provided with an answer to such criticisms.

I can conceive such objections becoming a source of very real perplexity even to good men, who are not able to solve them by any observations of their own, and have no right understanding of the position of Catholics towards the Bible. Are we bound, they may ask, to believe with Mr. Burgon or some Protestant commentator that "every book of it, every chapter of it, every verse of it, every word of it, every syllable of it, (where are we to stop?) every letter of it—is the direct utterance of the Most High, absolutely faultless and unerring"? Or may we believe with Stanley that there may be "errors in chronology, exaggerations in numbers, contradictions between the narratives"? When a Catholic comes with such questions as these, not captiously or in a spirit of unbelief, but only perplexed, tempted, and sincerely anxious to be "ready always to satisfy every one that asks him a reason of the hope which is in him," (1 Peter iii. 15,) I think he both requires and deserves a particular as well as a general answer. I should put before such a man, first the Canon of the Council of Trent on the subject of the Scriptures. This only declares that all the Books of the Bible as they are wont to be read in the Catholic Church and are in the old Vulgate Latin Edition, are to be held as sacred and canonical; "*the whole of these Books with all their parts;*" and I should explain to him that the most probable interpretation of these last words is that they have reference to those

portions of Scripture about which there had formerly been
some doubt in the Church and some of which were at that
very time rejected by the various sects of Protestants; some
part of the Book of Daniel, for example, the last twelve
verses of the Gospel of St. Mark, part of the eighth chapter
of St. John, &c. Next, I would go on to show him that the
Church had really defined very little as to the nature and
extent of the Divine inspiration of the Scriptures; but that
she certainly does not impose upon us a belief in their *verbal*
inspiration,* as though the sacred penmen had been mere
instruments of the Holy Spirit, contributing nothing whatever
of their own; whereas, on the other hand, it is no less certain, according to the teaching of all Catholic theologians,
that they were supernaturally protected from falling into any
mistake or error in their writings; moreover, that those
writings have come down to us, if not in their absolute in-
tegrity, yet at least without any corruption in things apper-
taining to the substance of what was written.† I say, apper-
taining to the *substance* of what was written, because no one
maintains that all the transcribers of Holy Scripture were
miraculously preserved from making a single mistake in
copying a list of names, for example, or a number of figures; and
there are not wanting perhaps two or three examples where
the presence of *some* kind of error seems undeniable, as for
instance in 2 Kings x. 18, compared with 1 Paralip. xix. 18.
In the one place we read that David slew of the Syrians the
men of seven hundred chariots, in the other seven thousand.
Again, in 2 Paral. ix. 25, the Vulgate, and consequently our
Douay Version, puts the number of Solomon's horses at
forty thousand, whereas the Hebrew (and English Protestant
Version) has only four thousand. These are errors or " contradictions," which can perplex no man; they are isolated
numbers, which may be read either one way or the other
without injury to the main narrative, and the occasion of the
discrepancy can be easily imagined. There are other " contradictions" too, not to be found in Colenso, which admit of
explanation, not so readily, yet without any just suspicion;
e.g., the difference between the sums in 2 Kings xxiv. 24, and
in 1 Paral. xxi. 25, as to the price of Areuna's threshing-
floor. Fifty sicles of silver can scarcely have been substituted,
by an error of transcription, for six hundred sicles of gold; but
there seems no valid objection to the explanation which is given

---

* The theological reader will understand here the necessary qualifications and
exceptions, as to the forms of the sacraments, &c.

† Perrone de loc. Theol. Pars. 11. c. II.

in the note to the latter passage in the Douay Bible. And again, the discrepancies between the Jewish History in the Pentateuch, and the abridgment of that History in the speech of St. Stephen in the Acts of the Apostles (vii. 14). Theologians distinguish here between the *dicta* of the inspired writers themselves, and those of others which the inspired writers only repeat.* The former are absolutely and indisputably certain; the latter need not always be received as such. St. Stephen took his numbers from the Septuagint, which inserts in verse twenty of the forty-sixth chapter of Genesis the names of three sons and two grandsons of the sons of Joseph, not to be found in the Hebrew; and so gives seventy-five in verse twenty-seven instead of seventy. The other points of difference between the same narratives may be explained by supposing St. Stephen to refer to a different transaction from that which we read in Genesis xxxiii. 19, a transaction nowhere recorded in the Scriptures, but the memory of which was preserved by tradition; or it may be explained in any other way you prefer, provided only that you steer clear of the error of Erasmus, who denied altogether the inspiration of the historical portion of the Bible, and of Holden and others who thought it unnecessary to suppose that the sacred writers had always been secured from slight errors, such as might proceed from a defect of memory or of knowledge, in matters which did not affect doctrine. Of course not even those who once held these loose opinions would have admitted the extreme consequences to which Colenso's application of them would lead; but I think they would have found it difficult to build an efficient barrier against them upon their own foundations. The safest ground for Catholics to take in their defence of the Bible is the highest, and before long I suspect they will be left alone in the defence of it. Already a new word is coming into common use in the controversies of Protestants, one with another, a word which strikes at the very root of all Protestant belief; I mean the word *Bibliolatry*: they are now denouncing this new sin of their co-religionists quite as loudly as they used to denounce what they called the *Mariolatry* of Catholics; and when we remember the old Protestant watchword, " the Bible, the whole Bible, *and nothing but the Bible*," we may well tremble for the immediate future that lies before them. It is well we should provide betimes for the Babel of confusion that may be expected, lest any of our own people should be carried away by the rising flood of unbelief. Even Colenso's objections, old as they

* Patrizi, Comm. de SS. Divinis. Romæ. 1851.

are for the most part, and refuted by those who at the close of the last century entered the lists against Voltaire, cannot be safely despised, I think. It is true, as we have seen, that many of them are very superficial and unfair, so that an honest and intelligent enquirer will not be misled by them; yet some perhaps may be deceived even by these; and in others, the array of figures brought to bear on the subject is so imposing, and the arguments so plausible, that it requires some attention to detect the fallacy.

I must go on with my work, then, wearisome as it is, and proceed to that which seems in Colenso's judgment to be the "crowning impossibility" of the whole narrative, and yet to be the most essentially interwoven with every part of it; viz., the number of the children of Israel at the Exodus. Holy Scripture says that they were about "600,000 men on foot, besides children." (Exodus, xii. 37.) Colenso says, this is a plain impossibility; for that there were only fifty-one sons of the patriarchs who went down into Egypt; that they lived there only two hundred and fifteen years; that it was distinctly foretold, that they should come into the promised land "in the fourth generation" (Gen. xv. 16); that if we assign to each male in each of the three intervening generations an average of four and a half sons, (the average of the sons of Jacob themselves), this will give us in the fourth generation 4,923 men, or, if we add all the generations together and suppose that not one man had died, 6,311. Nay, go further still, and add the next generation, who however (he says) would be mostly children, and you will only have 22,154; or something less than a twentieth part of the Scriptural number.

It is impossible, I think, for anybody to read this summary of Colenso's arguments (which yet I believe to be perfectly fair) without detecting at once some fallacies; as, for instance, only four generations allowed to a period of two hundred and fifteen years, or more than fifty years to a generation. Let us see what Scripture itself has to say upon this point. We read (Gen. l. 22) that Joseph lived to see the children of Ephraim to the third generation; he saw also his great grandsons by Manasses. Now he was thirty-six years old before his sons were born (Gen. xli. 46-50), and only one hundred and ten when he died (Gen. l. 25). It follows therefore that there were four generations of the children of Israel living together, within seventy years of their first coming into Egypt; and there was room for more than three times this number in the whole period of their sojourn in that country, even if we take the shortest time that can be assigned to it, viz., two hundred and fifteen years; so that, proceeding only at the rate of increase allowed by Colenso himself, we shall have no difficulty in arriving at an infinitely larger number than is required. But do we not hereby annul the promise in Gen. xv. 16? By no means, for surely this promise is strictly fulfilled, if *any* of the fourth generation are living at the Exodus, which they certainly are; Moses and Aaron, for example.

But again, Colenso's calculation includes only the sons of Jacob; it takes no account of his servants, or retainers: and yet I do not see how we can suppose these to have been excluded. Colenso indeed says that he had none. But what then had become of them? He certainly *once* had some (Gen. xxxii. 5, 16); and ¦it was not likely that they would have been left behind to perish of hunger in Chanaan. Probably they are included under the title, "my father's house" as distinguished from "my brethren" in Gen. xlvi. 31. They would have been circumcised (Gen. xvii. 12, 23), and though not reckoned among the pure seed of Israel, would certainly have been among the number of "the fighting men," being reckoned with that particular tribe to which their masters belonged. Suppose Jacob and all his sons to have had no more of these retainers (servants born in the house) than his grandfather Abraham had when he rescued Lot, viz., 318 (Gen. xiv. 14); allow to these Colenso's moderate ratio of increase, and you have from these alone very nearly the whole number of men given in Exodus xii. 37.

Or look at the matter another way—What is the ordinary rate of increase in an agricultural population of pure morals, and where there are ample means of subsistence? Malthus, in his famous Essay upon this subject (pp. 5, 6), first tells us of some of the Northern States of America, in which the population was "found to double itself, for above a century and a half successively, in less than 25 years." Next, he speaks of other parts of the same country, where "the population has been found to double itself in fifteen years. Even this extraordinary rate of increase is probably short of the utmost power of population. According to a table of Euler, the period of doubling will be only twelve years and four-fifths. And this proportion, he goes on to say, "is not only a possible supposition, but has actually occurred for short periods in more countries than one." Finally, he quotes another authority, which "supposes a doubling possible in so short a time as 10 years." And he concludes, that we may be "perfectly sure that we are *far within the truth*" if we say that " population, when unchecked, goes on doubling itself every twenty-five years; this is a rate in which all concurring testimonies agree and which has been repeatedly ascertained to be from procreation only."

Now try to call to mind one of those sums which doubtless you were made to work in your youth, wherein a horse was offered at what seemed to your inexperience a merely nominal price—a farthing for the first nail in one of his shoes, a half-penny for the second, a penny for the third, and so on, increasing in a geometrical ratio—try, I say, to call to mind the exhorbitant sum which the price of your horse ultimately reached when valued at this rate, and you will be able to form some idea of the product of Jacob's family, beginning with 70 souls, doubling itself (say) in every fifteen years, and continuing to do so during a period of 215, or 230 years. I will not inflict the sum upon you; but, unless my Arithmetic deceives me, it would give us a product much nearer to the numbers recorded in Scripture, than to Colenso's calculation.

So then it appears that Colenso's "plain impossibility" becomes possible, or even probable, merely on *natural* principles, and *ordinary* arithmetical calculations! But this method of reasoning is not just to the subject in hand. The historical credibility of the numbers or other facts stated in the Pentateuch must be tested by the standard of its own assertions; and it distinctly claims for the children of Israel a *supernatural* ratio of increase. What else means the promise by God to Abraham of a vast increase of seed, that his seed should become a great nation? a promise repeated to Abraham, to Isaac, and to Jacob: (Gen. xii. 2, xv. 5, xvii. 6, xxii. 17, xxv. 23, xxviii. 14, xxxii. 12, xlvi. 3.) And does not the alarm and jealousy of the Egyptians testify to the fulfilment of this promise? How else could they say, " the people of the children of Israel are numerous and stronger than we?" (Exod. i. 9.) And the sacred historian says expressly that " the children of Israel increased and sprung up into multitudes, and growing exceedingly strong they filled the land."

With these facts before me, I confess I cannot understand the repeated assertions of Colenso that " there is not the slightest indication in the Bible" of any extraordinary rate of increase; of any extraordinary fecundity in the Hebrew women, &c. He even quotes the acknowledged *falsehoods* of the Egyptian midwives (Exod. i. 19.) as *reliable evidence* to the contrary! It seems to me inconceivable, how any but a most blindly prejudiced mind could fall into such blunders as these. The *devout* student of Holy Scripture must surely see in this history not contradictions and physical impossibilities, but on the contrary the most wonderful harmony and agreement between the natural and the supernatural. God had promised the seed of Abraham an extraordinary increase in the land of Egypt; and the land of Egypt was precisely that in which even *naturally* the human race was wont to increase and multiply with extraordinary rapidity. Witness the testimony of Aristotle (Hist. Anim. vii. 4), who says that " twins are *common* in Egypt; even three or four at a birth *not rare*." Witness the no less distinct statement of Pliny (Hist. Nat. vii. 3.) " for a woman to have more than three children at a birth is accounted a portent, *except in Egypt, ubi fœtifer potu Nilus amnis;*" and presently he mentions an old author as recording a birth of seven children at once in Egypt. Of course I do not wish to lay more stress upon these statements than they will bear; but I cannot overlook them altogether; and to my mind they suggest another instance of that beautiful law whereby the God of nature and of grace so often combines in harmonious action the powers both of the natural and the supernatural worlds for the accomplishment of His own purposes. But when I turn from this consideration to the study of Colenso's Arithmetic, I am struck not only by the cold heartless infidelity of his calculations, but also by the harsh, arbitrary, uncritical way in which he handles the sacred text in order to pervert it to his sense. To the promise of God he attaches no value, as if it were absolutely powerless to produce what it had foretold; the strong, glowing language of Holy Writ, expressing in so striking a manner the extraordinary multiplication of the children of Israel, he passes by as an idle poetical exaggeration; he will confine himself to facts and figures; 215 years was the probable period of the sojourn in Egypt; there were to be four generations of sojourners; 4½ sons is a fair average to allow to each individual; divide and multiply *secundum artem*, and you get 22,000 instead of 600,000. This then is the issue on the first plea, in the case of "Colenso versus Moses." Can any one affect to believe that Colenso has stated the case fairly, argued it correctly, and *proved* the impossibility which obliges him so unwillingly to abandon his belief in the historical credibility of the Pentateuch?

Let us take another point intimately connected with the first. It is the number of the first-born as stated in Numbers iii. 43. Colenso makes very merry over this item of the

Mosaic Arithmetic. 22,273 first-born males, on the one
hand; 600,000 fighting men of 20 years old and upwards, on
the other; add a proportionate number of old men and boys;
double the number, to establish the proper balance between
the two sexes; make all fair allowance for a probable number
of deaths, and now divide and distribute into families; and
you will arrive (under Colenso's guidance) at these startling
results; 1st, that only one man in ten among the children of
Israel had a wife and family: 2ndly, that every mother
amongst them had on an average between 80 and 90 children.
"If you cannot believe this," says Colenso, "you must give
up the Bible numbers as impossible; and if the Bible numbers are impossible, then the Pentateuch is no record of real
facts; it is not historically true." And since few persons,
I suppose, if any, could be found ready to accept those two
arithmetical statements, the prospect is sufficiently alarming
to all lovers of the Bible. Probably this *is* the greatest difficulty of all; at least *I* thought so, and if you had asked me for
a satisfactory explanation of it a fortnight ago, I could not have
given you one. I should have answered that I had no doubt
but that the numbers were *somehow* correct, though I could
not pretend to say how; for that Moses had simply recorded
the facts, without mentioning all the circumstances of the
case, that might have removed any apparent difficulty; that
he had given the numbers as so many facts of the history, all
of which was to be believed on the Divine Authority which
proposes it to our belief, not to be used as the data of some
arithmetical problem to try the powers of human ingenuity.
And I think a reasonable man would have found nothing
unreasonable in such a reply. He might have wished for
something more directly solving his difficulty, but he would
not have given up the Bible for the want of it. A few days
ago however I came across a pamphlet, by far the ablest I
have yet happened to see upon this whole controversy, which
contains a *direct* solution of Colenso's difficulty, at once simple and ingenious, and, as it seems to me, eminently probable. The pamphlet I refer to is by the Rev. C. Pritchard,*
late fellow of St. John's College, Cambridge, and Secretary of
the Royal Astronomical Society; a mathematician therefore
and a man of figures, like Colenso himself, and when "Greek
meets Greek, then comes the tug of war." Mr. Pritchard
first lays down the same axiom as I myself insisted upon in
my first letter, viz., that if he can shew on any not violently

* Vindiciæ Mosaicæ. London: Bell and Daldy.

improbable hypothesis that the Scriptural numbers are possible, *Colenso's argument is destroyed*. Of course it is ; Colenso has undertaken to *force* all reasoning and calculating men to give up the belief they have hitherto had in the Bible, on the score of the utter *impossibility* of its arithmetical statements. Anything short of this will not fulfil his purpose. If then some hypothesis can be invented, barely possible, i.e. not contradicted by the text of the Sacred narrative itself, and not on any other account inadmissible, by the acceptance of which those statements can be made to appear, if not true, yet at least possible, the old belief in the Bible remains unshaken. Such an hypothesis Mr. Pritchard has invented in the present instance. He conjectures, or assumes by way of argument, that as the first-born males were set aside for the service of God and this was the only reason wherefore their census was taken, none would have been reckoned in this number, but those who were of the *pure* stock of Israel, the real children of the promise ; the sons of the strangers, the servants and retainers of all kinds, though rightly numbered among the fighting men, might perhaps have been rigidly excluded from this religious privilege. Observe, he does not say that it *was* so, but that it *may have been* so ; and that if it was, this circumstance would at once account for the paucity of the numbers. It is idle therefore to object that no traces of such a distinction can be found in the words of Moses ; is it *excluded* by the words of Moses ? Moses wrote, briefly and without explanation, first one fact and then another, just as they really occurred and as the Holy Spirit inspired him to write them, without caring to fit them together and smooth down apparent discrepancies between them. Thucydides and Herodotus, or any other ordinary historian, would not have dared to leave such glaring inconsistencies on the very surface of their narrative ; Moses could afford to do it, because his work was not to be tried by the canons of a merely human criticism; but if any one chooses so to try it and thus creates difficulties for himself and others, it is surely unreasonable to refuse a solution of those difficulties, merely because it rests on some hypothesis, which is beside or beyond, not against, the *littera scripta* of the Mosaic record.

I cannot leave Mr. Pritchard's conjectural explanation of this particular difficulty as to the number of the first-born, without observing how happily it explains another of Colenso's perplexities, viz. Whence comes it that, whereas the posterity of Dan and Juda, having but one son each, increased and

multiplied to sixty or seventy thousand, the posterity of Levi,
who had three sons, does not much exceed twenty-two thousand, i.e. does not come up to a fourth part of the average
numbers of the other tribes? and still further, that these
twenty-two thousand had only increased by a single thousand
during thirty-eight years of the wanderings in the wilderness?
(See Numbers ii. 26, iii. 39, xxvi. 42, 62.) Both these anomalies are at once explained, if we concede Mr. Pritchard's
hypothesis, which is at least probable, viz. that in the numbering of the other tribes the children of servants, strangers,
or of mixed marriages were not excluded, but that in the
numbering of this, the sacred tribe, greater strictness was
observed, none but the pure stock of Levi being admitted.
And any mind, accustomed to the weighing of moral evidence, must needs acknowledge, that an hypothesis which
thus grasps and links together facts not obviously dependent
on one another, bears a strong stamp of truth.

Another " self-contradiction" Colenso imagines himself to
have found, in comparing the extent of the promised land
with the number of the chosen people who were to possess it,
and with the reason assigned by God for the *gradual* exter-
mination of its original inhabitants. We read in the Book
of Exodus (xxiii. 29) that God said "I will not cast them
out from thy face in one year, lest the land be brought into a
wilderness, and the beasts multiply against thee." Upon
this Colenso (or one of his admirers) exclaims that we have
here the very " climax of inconsistency between the facts and
figures" of the Bible narrative. He says that if all the
inhabitants of the land had been driven out at once, the Israelites alone would have sufficed to people the country as thickly
as two or three English counties which he mentions, and which
certainly are in no danger of being " brought into a wilderness ;" or again, he says that the population would have been
nearly twenty times as thick as it now is in Natal, and yet
that the strongest of the wild beasts have been already extir-
pated, and that others are disappearing from that colony.
How then could there have been any real danger from the
multiplication of the beasts in Judea?

It seems strange that any student should have overlooked
the altered relations between man and beast which are the
result of modern inventions. Had the colonists of Natal
only the same means of contending with the wild beasts as
Samson had, when " a young lion met him raging and roar-
ing," he "having nothing at all in his hand," (Judges xiv. 6,)
or as David (1 Kings xvii. 35) when the lion and the bear

came against his father's sheep, and "he caught them by the throat, and strangled and killed them," we may be allowed to doubt whether "the strongest of the wild beasts" would have been so soon exterminated. Moreover, recent travellers tell us that at this very moment, the Holy Land, having a population about equal to the number of the Israelites when they took possession of it, suffers very considerable inconvenience from the incursions of wild beasts; now, as in the days of the prophets of old, wild boars often destroy the grain and other produce of the land along the banks of the Jordan, bears destroy whole vineyards on the sides of the Anti-Lebanon in a single night, and jackals may be seen dragging corpses from their shallow graves under the very walls of Jerusalem.*

So says one who has entered the lists against Colenso, giving his name and stating that these are facts within his own knowledge and observation. He adds that three-fourths of the richest and best portion of the country remain uncultivated and desolate.

This same traveller makes another observation also which is worth repeating, with reference to Colenso's description of the camp, as one vast mass of tents, "not much inferior in compass, we must suppose, to London"—(*Must we suppose* its parks, squares, palaces, theatres, churches and museums to be included in this measurement?)—He says that nobody who has ever travelled in the East would have fallen into this error; that he himself once rode for two days straight forward through the flocks of a section of an Arab tribe in the same locality, tended by swarms of men and women, boys and girls, while the encampment of the chief was at that very moment distant not less than thirty miles, at right angles to the traveller's course.

This picture helps also to dispel another difficulty with which Colenso has amused himself from the injunction in Deut. xxiii. 13., even if it were not sufficiently disposed of by the first words of the ninth verse, which seem so clearly to limit its application to a military camp in time of war. I should not have alluded to this subject but for the sake of calling attention to the remarkable fact (mentioned by one of Colenso's critics) that the "Punjaub Sanitary Report for 1862," actually recommends the practice of the natives in these matters in preference to European habits, as being best suited to the climate, and observes that it is "in strict accord-

* Athenæum, January 17, 1863.

D

ance with the Divine ordinance which was given to the first great camp the world ever saw."

But enough; I must not try your patience too long; and indeed my own is now well-nigh exhausted. I have followed Colenso through at least nine-tenths of his difficulties and "contradictions"; and I think I have laid down principles which will suffice for the solution of any that remain. Critics of his school may object to some of the explanations that have been given as far-fetched and improbable. This is a matter of opinion, in which I should differ from them; but at any rate it can hardly be maintained that the explanations are impossible, and unless this can be proved, Colenso's argument is destroyed. Indeed, more than once in his book, he himself acknowledges with reference to some of these explanations, or others like them, that they might be accepted, *if* the historical character of the Pentateuch were established. Now this is precisely the standpoint in which we have the advantage over him; we know and are sure on the declaration of competent authority that the Pentateuch is divinely inspired and contains a true history. We are not therefore easily staggered by any apparent difficulties; we are ready to accept this or that probable conjecture which supplies a means of solving them, or if we cannot solve them at all, we are not much concerned. We believe all the facts recorded, though we may not be able to combine and reconcile them. We agree with Colenso in holding that a volume of inspired truth cannot relate as facts physical impossibilities, but we fail to find in the Mosaic Books those physical impossibilities which he imagines he detects there. There is only one Biblical statement that I know of, objected by Colenso, which could be rightly so described, and this is the statement in Genesis xlv. 12, which occupies therefore the very foremost place in his van-guard, but which I have reserved until now for my own greater convenience.

We read in Genesis xlvi. 6, that "Jacob came into Egypt with all his seed, his sons and grandsons, daughters, and all his offspring together. And these are the names of the children of Israel that entered into Egypt, he and his children. ......The sons of Juda, Her and Onan, and Sela and Phares, and Zara. And Her and Onan died in the land of Chanaan. And sons were born to Phares, *Hesron and Hamul.*" The insertion of these two last names seems to involve a physical impossibility. For Hesron and Hamul were the sons of Phares, and Phares was himself the son of Thamar by her incestuous connection with Juda, after she had become the widow of Juda's eldest and second sons, and been refused to (or by) his third son. In other words, they were Juda's grandsons, but they stood (so far as *time* is concerned) in the relation of *great*-grandsons to Juda. How then is it possible that they could have been born in Chanaan and *gone down into Egypt* with Juda, since Juda himself could not at that time have been more than forty-four years old at the most? It is a "plain physical impossibility," says Colenso, and we quite agree with him in thinking so. How then are we to explain it?

An attempt has been made indeed to alter the statement of this sum. It has been alleged that there is nothing in the Sacred Text to fix the age of Juda; that he may have been much older perhaps. This does not seem to me to alter the case at all. The date of Juda's *marriage*, not his age, is the point on which everything depends; and the date of this *is* fixed, I think, with tolerable accuracy. For Juda married presently after the sale of Joseph; so we gather from Genesis xxxviii. 1.* Now Joseph was sixteen *before* he was sold (chap. xxxvii. 2.); and he was thirty years old when he stood before Pharaoh (xli. 46). Add to these fourteen, the seven years of plenty and not more than two of the scarcity (chap. xlv. 11.) before Jacob went down into Egypt, and you have about twenty-three years in all (14 + 7 + 2). And it is clearly impossible within these limits to find time for Juda's marriage, the birth of his three sons, their marriages (or quasi-marriages) with Thamar, the birth of Phares of this Thamar, and finally, the birth of Hesron and Hamul, the two sons of Phares.

We feel the difficulty quite as fully as Colenso himself, and one or two other difficulties also, connected with the same subject; and yet we cannot admit that they at all disturb our faith in the historical credibility of the Pentateuch. Thus, it is a difficulty in the same narrative, that ten sons are attributed to Benjamin, who cannot have been more than twenty-two years old at the time; yet Colenso gets over this, by supposing that he had many wives! Again, the number of souls that went down into Egypt is in the Hebrew and Vulgate stated to be seventy; in the Septuagint version of this same passage, it is seventy-five; and St. Stephen, the

---

* Lightfoot and others after him have contended that the expression "*at that time*" need not be interpreted strictly as a chronological note. To those who agree with the Talmudists that there is no chronological order in the Pentateuch, this observation may commend itself. Most Catholic theologians however agree, I suppose, with Patrizi (Comment. de Script. Div. Rome, 1851) that in the historical books the *order* of events "ad inspirationem pertinere." (p. 18).

Proto-Martyr, in his abridgment of the Jewish History addressed to the council in Jerusalem, adopts this larger number (Acts vii. 14). The whole subject therefore is beset with difficulties, and has engaged the attention of commentators on Holy Scripture from St. Augustin downwards. I need not repeat their explanations. I will only observe two things : 1st, that it is undeniable—explain it how you will—that the Sacred Text itself says of two persons in this list of Jacob's family, *both* that they were " *born in* Egypt," *and* that they " *entered into* Egypt," or came down into it. I am speaking of the two sons of Joseph, and referring to chap. xlvi. 27. There we read that Ephraim and Manasses were born in Egypt, and yet they go to make up the number of seventy, of whom we read that they came down into Egypt. Now, if this can be said of Ephraim and Manasses, why not of Hesron and Hamul also ? and what right has Colenso to insist upon it " that the writer here means to say that Hesron and Hamul were born in the land of Canaan because he says they came into Egypt with Jacob," when he cannot possibly have meant to say this of the other two (since he distinctly testifies the contrary), concerning whom he nevertheless has made the same statement ?

And my second observation is this ; that a careful study of the text itself seems to reveal a marked distinction between the historian's way of mentioning these two pairs of brothers, and the way in which all the others of the seventy are named. Ordinarily, the names are given, succeeding one another as in a catalogue, without the use of any verb at all ; but at the end of verse twelve the writer abandons this brevity, and says, " and sons *were born* to Phares, Hesron and Hamul." In like manner in verse twenty, we read, "And sons were born to Joseph." This peculiarity of expression leads us to suspect some distinction present to the mind of the historian between these persons, and the general mass of those named in the catalogue; and it belongs, in the Hebrew* and in our translation, only to those two cases, where the facts of the history render it imperative upon us to suppose that there *was* some distinction. Moreover it is very remarkable that in the Septuagint, the same peculiarity belongs to *one* other set of names ; that, namely, in which we have already seen cause to suspect some latent error, the ten sons of Benjamin. Here the Septuagint catalogue gives us only *three* sons of Benjamin ;

---

* The Hebrew verb is not "were born," but simply "*were*." The difference is immaterial to the argument, which rests on the presence of any verb at all in these cases, when there is none in the rest of the catalogue.

then it adds, " there were born to " one of these sons, five or
six sons, and lastly, it mentions one of a still later generation,
the great-grandson of Benjamin. I say then, that this peculiarity of expression, attaching *only* to those of whom we feel
confident that they could not really have been born in Chanaan and gone down into Egypt, is a very clear indication that
the writer was as conscious of this fact as we are, and that he
meant to set a chronological mark of distinction upon them.
But why then did he name them at all ? and why did he
reckon them in the number of those who went down into
Egypt? I do not pretend to know. Many reasons have been
suggested by various commentators; some more, some less
satisfactory; as, for instance, that the names are inserted as a
kind of compensation for Her and Onan, whose deaths have
been just recorded : or that there was some special excellency
or eminence in them over the rest of Jacob's grandsons, as
there was in Ephraim and Manasses (Gen. xlviii. 5.), &c. &c.
Perhaps none of the reasons assigned is altogether conclusive.
Nevertheless I do not on this account abandon my belief in
the historical truthfulness of the inspired narrative ; any more
than hundreds and thousands before me, who have examined
the same difficulty and been equally unable thoroughly to
satisfy themselves with a solution. For it must be remem-
bered that this, like most of Colenso's difficulties, has been
patent to every student of Holy Writ from generation to
generation ; and may we not justly suspect some perversion of
the will, or of the understanding, in a writer who thinks that
he can upset the belief of the wisest and best of mankind for
the last two thousand years, merely by means of a few arithmetical or genealogical difficulties of this kind, which have
challenged the attention of critics, whether friends or foes,
during the whole of this period, yet without impairing the belief of the Christian world in the Divine authority of the Books
containing them ?
And now I must take my leave of Colenso. He has robbed
me of some hours that were claimed by other duties, and I am
afraid my letters will bear many tokens of the haste and in-
terruptions amid which they have been written. Their materials too (like those of the walls of Athens, of which Thucydides tells us) have been taken from all sides, from public and
from private sources, without scruple ; and after all, the subject is not really ended ; on the contrary it is only begun, for
on this very day I see that a second volume of his work has
issued from the press, and is to be followed by a third.
Nevertheless I believe it will be worth while to publish what I

have written, because I have reason to know that even such a
reply as this may be of service to some. I make no apology
to *you* for the popular unlearned way in which I have answered
your enquiry. You did not ask for your own sake, but that
you might have a ready answer to give to others. Colenso
has written for the unlearned, and I have wished to keep the
same class in view in what I have said in reply. They are the
larger and more necessitous class, and no one, so far as I can
hear, among Catholic writers has announced his intention of
doing anything for their protection and assistance. Meanwhile the plague is raging round them ; they are living in a
poisoned atmosphere, and they require some antidote to pre-
serve them from the infection. May God bless these feeble
efforts for their good.

Yours ever very sincerely in Christ,

S. N.

LETTER V.

Dear Doctor,

Many thanks for your *work*, which (as I said in my
former letter) will be most useful to me ; and all the more so
as I should never have had the patience to do it myself. We
are pretty well agreed as to how the controversy with unbelievers should be conducted. The combination of your argument with mine will prove a two-edged sword with which I
hope, when occasion offers, to do battle manfully against the
enemy. I have only one thing to add (if you will have
patience with me) to what I have said already, and that is that
supposing Dr. Colenso to be in good faith (upon which you
throw some doubt), no Protestant has a right, on Protestant
principles, to find fault with his opinion, or interfere with
him for expressing it. Judging him from the Catholic
Stand-point Colenso is wrong, for we hold to an objective
standard of truth ; but Protestantism offers him the Sacred
Book, which he reads, as he reads it, like the rest of them ;
and, whatever comes of it, is thereby a true Protestant. And
after all, it is not to be wondered at that, since they differ
amongst themselves, he should differ from the rest of them.
For here Dr. Newman's remark is very pertinent, that where
each man's mind is made the standard of truth it would be

unreasonable to expect a common standard. They may say
that Dr. Colenso's conclusion is a wrong one, if they choose;
but when all is said, his wisdom is not their wisdom, and as
a true Protestant, he must go by his own lights, and not by
theirs. The simple fact that they disagree with one another is
the grand condemnation of their condemnation. No: this
crop of unbelief which has sprung up in our days is the legi-
timate produce of Protestantism itself, which gives a man
with prayer and the Bible to make a religion for himself.
(You see I am on my old line of rail again.) The wonder is,
not that the last result should have at length appeared, but
that it did not appear long before. What is it that makes a
principle germinate with such fungus-like rapidity on the
Continent and so slowly with us? Anyhow there was a stag-
nancy in English Protestantism before the time of Dr.
Arnold; whereas since his time (owing I suppose to German
influences) the pace has become so rapid that one must read
hard to keep up with it. And now every variety of unbelief
is rife within the bosom of the Establishment. But since
this is the case, is there not some unfairness in the outcry
raised by Protestants against Dr. Colenso as though he were
the only offender, while it is allowed to Professor Stanley to
indoctrinate the youth of Oxford with the very same principles
of Biblical Criticism? Is it a greater sin to say with the
former that there are contradictions in the Pentateuch, or with
the latter that one must not enter into too close a scrutiny of
the history of Samson? But if on the other hand Colenso
alone is to be held up to obloquy as the wolf within the fold,
can that really be the true fold of Christ which is unable
to cast out the wolf? Truly it was an awkward confession
which had to be made by the Bishop of Rochester, in the
address to his clergy, that nothing remains but to pray for
Dr. Colenso. Allow me to exhibit the course these gentlemen
have taken in this matter in the form of

A FABLE.

Once upon a time, the wolf disguised himself as a shepherd
and made sad work among the sheep and tender lambs of the
flock. Whereupon, the sheep and shepherds of the neigh-
bouring flocks were sore afraid; and a council was called to
determine what were best to be done. There was a great deal
of talking, but, as no one dared to act, it seemed that nothing
would come of it. At last, one old shepherd, bolder than the
rest, sent a message to the wolf, begging him to withdraw back

to the woods, for that his presence was injurious to the flock. The wolf laughed, on receiving the message. "My friend," he answered back, "you consider this matter from a sheepish point of view: were you in my place, you would think otherwise." When the wolf's answer was delivered, the old shepherd thus addressed the assembly. "My Brothers," he said, "it seems that remonstrance is vain. It is my advice that, seeing this wild creature must still remain a shepherd, we pray Jove that he would deign to change the nature of the beast, and give him a distaste for mutton."

I remain,

Dear Doctor,

Yours affectionately,

C. M.

PRINTED BY RICHARDSON AND SON, DERBY.

www.ingramcontent.com/pod-product-compliance
Lightning Source LLC
Chambersburg PA
CBHW031803090426
42739CB00008B/1140